Copyright © 2024 by Cindy Rinne. All rights reserved.
Published by Nauset Press
nausetpress.com

No part of this book may be reproduced or transmitted in any form without written permission from the publisher, except by reviewers, who may quote brief excerpts in connection with a review.

Cover and Book Design: Nauset Press

Photography Copyright © 2024 Heather Rinne
Sculpture Copyright © 2024 A.E. Van Fleet
Chapter Opening Images: Public Domain: *Color Field Studies: Chromolithographs* by the artist Eduard Pechuel-Loesche showing the sky after the Krakatao volcano eruption in 1883.
ISBN: 978-1-962890-02-1

Disclaimer: This book is not meant to replace professional care. Please seek the advice of a physician or other qualified health care provider if you need medical or psychological help. The book is not meant to forecast or provide information with absolute certainty. The information is not to be counted as legal, medical, or psychological advice. There are no guarantees and the author, artists, and publisher are not accountable for any interpretations or decisions made by the reader.

DANCING THROUGH THE FIRE DOOR

GUIDED JOURNEYS IN ART AND POETRY

BY
CINDY RINNE

PHOTOGRAPHS BY
HEATHER RINNE

SCULPTURES BY
A.E. VAN FLEET

NAUSET PRESS
WAREHAM, MASSACHUSETTS

TABLE OF CONTENTS
(ITALICS DENOTE IMAGES THROUGHOUT THE CONTENTS)

HOW TO USE THE GUIDEBOOK 8
GUIDED JOURNEYS 9
INTRODUCTION: BACKSTORY. 10
PUBLISHER'S NOTE 11

KEYWORDS

CHAPTER ONE: JOURNEY . . . 13

WATER GOES WHERE IT WISHES	15	CLEANSE
MESSAGES ARRIVE	16	WITNESS
DEAR ROUGH EMERALD, ...	17	DREAMS
IRIS CYCLES	18	INNER STRENGTH
HOPE INTUITION REBIRTH	19	OPEN HEART
REST OR WALK.	20	GRACE
DEAR BODY, ...	21	SURRENDER
A PIONEER.	22	AWAKE
FRIENDS HUG	23	RADIANCE
SELF DOUBT ERASED.	24	CEREMONY
BEAR GODDESS.	25	WISDOM
WATERS TO SPRINKLE UPON MY OFFERING	26	GENUINE
SELF-FORGIVENESS	28	OVERCOME
TREE OF LIFE	29	MEDITATE
DANCING THROUGH THE FIRE DOOR . . .	30	TRANSFORM
FALL IN LOVE WITH MYSELF	31	GENTLE
MARKERS OF TIME	32	TRUST
NATURE'S ALCHEMY	33	GUIDANCE
BELLY CRY	34	DARING
ANGEL	35	PREPARE

CHAPTER TWO: AURA 37

		KEYWORDS
WATER GOES WHERE IT WISHES II	38 . . .	.SEASON
SPARKS UP HER SPINE	39 . . .	.RESILIENCE
A PROTECTIVE AURA	40 . . .	.RECONNECT
FIRE IN HER BELLY	41 . . .	.STRENGTH
TRANSITIONS	42 . . .	.PASSION
DISCORD WITH PLANTS AND ANIMALS . .	42 . . .	.SPEAK OUT
OF BEDROCK AND BONE	43 . . .	.CHALLENGE
OF BEDROCK AND BONE II.	44 . . .	.MIST
ANSWERS WILL COME	45 . . .	.DEVOTION
GROWTH OF TALENTS	46 . . .	.DESTINY
CONNECTED	47 . . .	.KINDNESS
FLOWS IN HER VEINS.	48 . . .	.FLAME
ASTRAL BODY	48 . . .	.CHANGE
FELDSPAR	49 . . .	.ENERGY
TIME MEANS NOTHING.	49 . . .	.OMENS
I MUST RETURN	50 . . .	.ROUGH
REMEMBER	50 . . .	.REBIRTH
AQUAMARINE	51 . . .	.PORTAL
AMETHYST	52 . . .	.GO FORWARD
MERMAID AS MAP	53 . . .	.REGENERATE
WHAT DOES THIS ACHE NEED.	54 . . .	.COCOON
WARMING	55 . . .	.PERSPECTIVE
STABILITY	56 . . .	.ROOTED
CHANT FOR SEEDS TO GROW	56 . . .	.REACH
SLOW MOVEMENTS	57 . . .	.ALCHEMY
PUT INTO PLACE	57 . . .	.NEW PATH
SNOW-CHILLED BONES.	58 . . .	.UNIQUE
NEW LIFE	58 . . .	.SOLACE
SCAN THE HORIZON	59 . . .	.SERENE
DEAR SNOWY OWL, ...	59 . . .	.WIND
SECRETS OF WHAT MATTERS	60 . . .	.TIMING
DEAR SNOWY OWL, II.	61 . . .	.SACRED
EARTH.	62 . . .	.GROUND
FIRE.	62 . . .	.GROW
WATER.	63 . . .	.TIDES
AIR	64 . . .	.FLY
DEAR SNOWY OWL, III	65 . . .	.SLOWING

CHAPTER THREE: TOME 67

Title	Page	Keyword
WATER GOES WHERE IT WISHES III	68	COMFORT
SOUND WAVES WASH	69	HIDDEN
SPIRAL OPEN	70	TENDERNESS
GARNET MOON	71	SPIRAL
BREATH AS VIBRATION	72	REFLECT
FUTURE SELF	72	GAZE
SECRETS OF THE DARK	73	SPEAK
HERBS TO HEAL	73	FRIEND
SOUNDSCAPES	74	LISTEN
THE WORLD BREATHES ME	75	SUBTLE
WHISPER WHAT WAS	75	VULNERABLE
BODY NEEDS REPAIR	76	WAIT
VOCAL MEMORIES	76	SONG
I AM MORE THAN MY BODY	77	HEAL
AURA SHIFTS	78	SAFE
ADORNED WITH STARS	78	VISIBLE
SHE WANDERS	79	COURAGE
GARDEN OF CALM	80	ACTION
GARDEN OF CALM II	81	LEARN
BORN OF WATER AND WIND	82	THIRST
SHE DIRECTS ME	82	FOCUS
CRYSTALS NO FACETS	83	DIVINE
GARDEN OF CALM III	83	PEACE
REVEAL TIGER, PEACOCK, OR LOTUS	84	SIGNS
NATURE AND SIMPLICITY	85	HARMONY
DEAR FLEETING LIFE,	86	CREATIVITY
HOW TO UNDERSTAND	87	LOYALTY
WRITE A STORY	87	PLAY
LIGHT AND SHADOW SIDES	88	DUALITY
SHE OVERSEES	88	FLOW
ROSE, GODDESS, BEE, MOON	89	PRESENT
WOVE MEDICINE	90	RISKS
IX CHEL	91	DESIRE
THUNDER SPIRIT PORTAL	92	EXPECTATION
RUMBLED WISDOM	92	INSPIRE
ELECTRIFYING SHIFTS	93	MOVEMENT

KEYWORDS

CHAPTER FOUR: EVOLVE 95

Title	Page	Keyword
FLUID VOICE	96	PERMISSION
WATER GOES WHERE IT WISHES IV	97	SUBCONSCIOUS
IN THE BELLY OF A CANOE	98	PILGRIMAGE
MAP UNFOLDS	99	UNCLUTTER
SUDDENLY WASHED	99	UNDERTOW
POINT THE PROW	101	GIFTS
SAFE RETURN	102	NOURISH
SENSE THE HEARTBEAT	103	RECOVERY
HOME: WINTER CROSSROADS	104	FIERY ENERGY
LETTING GO	105	CLEARING
ACROSS THE CANYON	106	CRASH
RELEASE	108	ADJUST
SUN IN MY HORNS	108	PROTECT
THIS THRESHOLD	109	INTENTION
GIFT GIVER	110	UNCONDITIONAL
SOLSTICE DARK	111	HONEST
DEEP TIME	111	LINEAGE
COLLECTIVE MEMORY	112	QUIET
PLACE MY PALMS	112	CONNECT
SELECT ANOTHER POSSIBILITY	113	CONVERSATION
SUBLIME MESSAGES	114	RESPECT
LANDSCAPE INSIDE MOTHER EARTH	116	RITUAL
CHAPARRAL RESURGENCE	117	BREATHE
MY RIBS OPEN	118	CONJURE
LUNGS OF SILENT WATERS	118	ALIGN
FRESHNESS EXPLODES	119	HOPE
HOLDS A PAST LIFE	119	RECHARGE
UNDER BLOOD MOON	120	LOST
ACCEPT DAY AND NIGHT	121	CENTER
LUNAR WISDOM	121	NATURE
VIEW DOWN THE PATH	122	AFFINITY
VIEW DOWN THE PATH II	123	RELAX

		KEYWORDS
EPILOGUE 125		
PAUSE 126	. . . . .	SHRINE
MANY NAMES 127	. . . . .	SYMPATHY
SMOKY PRAYER 128	. . . . .	GLOW
HEALING SPRINGS 129	. . . . .	BLOOM
MARK TIME 130	. . . . .	RUMINATE
DIGEST DOUBTS 131	. . . . .	MEMORIES
FIRESTONES OF FEAR 131	. . . . .	ACCUMULATION
CHARMS THE WIND 132	. . . . .	OBJECTS
DECIDES TO FORGET 132	. . . . .	IDENTITY
BEGINNING AGAIN 133	. . . . .	DISCERN
NOTES AND ACKNOWLEDGMENTS 134		
ARTIST BIOGRAPHIES 135		

HOW TO USE THIS GUIDEBOOK

Every page contains a poem or image(s). Each poem and image has an associated keyword, in color. The image titles, shown in the gutter credits, contain fragments from the poems. Possibility comes in affirmation, challenge, inspiration, and insight.

You can choose a page at random to prepare you for the day. Read the title(s) and key word(s) for that page. Read the poem or view the images. Images are a type of language. Spend some time with the pages to see what resonates with you. Record your experience in a journal. Sometimes the message is a confirmation. Or you might not understand the message right away. Date the journal entry and check back.

Another option is to follow the *Guided Journeys* on the following page. Discover a theme or message within the journey. Explore inner and outer realms.

However you choose a page, be present with the poem and image(s). Does a word or phrase stand out? Is there something in the image that catches your attention? Perhaps research additional meanings for an animal, goddess, plant, tree. Meditate on the key word. Write down your thoughts, discoveries, or questions.

GUIDED JOURNEYS

CHAPTER ONE: JOURNEY

- **PATHWAY:** CLEANSE 15 | WITNESS 16 | OVERCOME 28 | PREPARE 35
- **ANCESTORS:** SURRENDER 21 | WISDOM 25 | CEREMONY 24
- **OTTER:** DREAMS 17 | GRACE 20 | GENUINE 26
- **GODDESS:** INNER STRENGTH 18 | RADIANCE 23 | AWAKE 22 | GENTLE 31
- **BODY:** OPEN HEART 19 | MEDITATE 29 | TRANSFORM 30 | TRUST 32

CHAPTER TWO: AURA

- **GUIDES:** PASSION, SPEAK OUT 42 | ENERGY, OMENS 49 | PERSPECTIVE 55
- **COURAGE:** STRENGTH 41 | CHALLENGE 43 | ROOTED, REACH 56
- **TREASURE:** SEASON 38 | RESILIENCE 39 | COCOON 54 | SACRED 61 | TIMING 60
- **RITUAL:** RECONNECT 40 | ROUGH, REBIRTH 50 | SLOWING 65
- **HORIZONS:** KINDNESS 47 | PORTAL 51 | GO FORWARD 52

CHAPTER 3: TOME

- **GRIEF:** COMFORT 68 | SPIRAL 71 | COURAGE 79 | MOVEMENT 93
- **MEMORY:** REFLECT, GAZE 72 | SUBTLE, VULNERABLE 75 | DESIRE 91
- **WISDOM:** SPEAK, FRIEND 73 | LISTEN 74 | DIVINE, PEACE 83
- **SILENCE:** WAIT, SONG 76 | HEAL 77 | SIGNS 84 | PRESENT 89
- **WILDERNESS:** LEARN 81 | THIRST, FOCUS 82 | CREATIVITY 86 | RISKS 90

CHAPTER 4: EVOLVE

- **IDENTITY:** PERMISSION 96 | SUBCONSCIOUS 97 | HOPE, RECHARGE 119 | AFFINITY 122
- **STRUGGLE:** PILGRIMAGE 98 | UNCLUTTER, UNDERTOW 99 | RITUAL 116 | CONJURE, ALIGN 118
- **HEALING:** GIFTS 101 | RECOVERY 103 | UNCONDITIONAL 110 | QUIET, CONNECT 112 | RELAX 123
- **WITNESS:** NOURISH 102 | CONVERSATION 113 | CENTER, NATURE 121
- **RELEASE:** FIERY ENERGY 104 | ADJUST, PROTECT 108 | INTENTION 109 | LOST 120

EPILOGUE

- **REST:** SHRINE 126 | SYMPATHY 127 | GLOW 128 | BLOOM 129
- **DIARY:** RUMINATE 130 | MEMORIES, ACCUMULATION 131 | DISCERN 133

INTRODUCTION: BACKSTORY

My house burned in 2003. Even the windows melted. The loss was contained in my body as back spasms. The fear of fire strong. Many years later I decided it was time for a new iteration of self. To befriend and integrate the fire. I danced with Pele, the Hawaiian goddess of volcanoes and fire, allowing her inside. Fire as volcano or basalt is a character in the book. Water remembers through all of existence. Water as womb as body. I accepted the healing and went forward. Water became a character as a nymph throughout the book as she evolves. This is a book of Water and Fire. Of Grief and Gratitude. A collaboration of a poet and two artists.

PUBLISHER'S NOTE

I began working with Cindy Rinne on *Dancing Through the Fire Door: Guided Journeys in Art and Poetry* in early 2023. She experienced the catastrophic loss of her home burning to the ground in the Southern Californian Old Fire in 2003. Her book is a two-decade healing manifestation of that loss. *Dancing Through the Fire Door* is a tome that has some roots in climate change with its attendant devastations. It is a book with a healing modality that could be helpful to people grappling with any trauma, cognitive dissonance, or surreal disassociation following disaster. One day, your sense of self and sanctuary is intact; the next day, loss upends everything. How do you rebuild? How do you process what happened to you?

Meditating, savoring beauty in the world, and accepting reality are cornerstones of Cognitive Behavior Therapy (CBT). Although Rinne is not a therapeutic or medical professional, her visionary expression in *Dancing Through the Fire Door* lands on these concepts in a way that spoke true to me. As I spent time laying out and designing her book, I became calmer while I worked on organizing the visual and text elements to amplify her healing messages.

The microcosm of tragedy affects the self. But the macrocosm of tragedy is informed by institutional choices that create multiple personal tragedies. Climate change is a macrocosm that continues to pressure humanity, and we must consider how to protect people by strategically rebuilding infrastructure to withstand unpredictable events, and learning to heal people by teaching resilience in an uncertain world. But the microcosm of tragedy, spanning the individual's interior life, must be treated by the individual. As shown by *Dancing Through the Fire Door*, there is value in creatively recording our emotional responses to grapple with our current reality — but also, hopefully, providing a template for future generations to understand and learn from while holding space to evolve through difficult circumstances. I hope you will find solace in this book.

Karyn Kloumann
Publisher, Nauset Press
Wareham, MA
August 23, 2023

CHAPTER ONE

JOURNEY

GUIDED JOURNEYS

- **PATHWAY:** CLEANSE 15 | WITNESS 16 | OVERCOME 28 | PREPARE 35
- **ANCESTORS:** SURRENDER 21 | WISDOM 25 | CEREMONY 24
- **OTTER:** DREAMS 17 | GRACE 20 | GENUINE 26
- **GODDESS:** INNER STRENGTH 18 | RADIANCE 23 | AWAKE 22 | GENTLE 31
- **BODY:** OPEN HEART 19 | MEDITATE 29 | TRANSFORM 30 | TRUST 32

Water Goes Where it Wishes

The Water Goddess dwells

inside a baobab tree.

She caresses the inner bark.

No tree rings. Spells cascade

from her hands

like a waterfall

pounds the earth. She names a nymph

JOURNEY

CLEANSE

WITNESS

MESSAGES ARRIVE

Dear Rough Emerald,

Waterfalls flow through me.

My chakras open.
Messages arrive from Wind,
Stones, Trees,
and Cloud-People—

Focus! We give you energy
for friendship,
success, and peace.

I lie on the sand and birth
planets to the rhythm
of the waves. You witness
my ritual as I transform
into the Enchantress.

You remind me to step back
from intimidation and become
grounded in the Earth of myself.
Encourage me to reach
for Grandfather Sun.

Clarity comes in a flood of ideas.
Dreams. My body spins
lost in a trance
as I listen to your
quiet heart.

You ask me to pay attention
to signs and omens
while the otter takes
me to the deep places
of unspoken wisdom.

DREAMS

Iris Cycles

*Soaring to heaven on balanced wings, [Iris] blazed
a rainbow trail beneath clouds as she flew.*

Virgil, Aeneid 9

I connect the core of my body to the center of the Earth
and become one with the hiddenness. I wait and develop
in secret soil. Bulbs settle   root just under surface.

After a long sleep, buds unfurl in watercolor hues—
blue   purple yellow. Iris petals awake as a divine link
between Heaven and Earth— psychic abilities   hope

intuition   rebirth. Then my body vanishes like the goddess Iris
as rainbow born in mists. A place between water and light.
Messenger goddess of golden wings   a herald's rod   water pitcher.

My iris eye chamber   decreases the pupil.
More light enters my sight.   I look around my space
it aligns with the universe.   Expand   contract   like the tides.

INNER STRENGTH

GRACE

REST OR WALK

Dear Body,

You carry me through many years—
injury, sickness, and birth pains.

Hair goes from dark brown
to gray. Wrinkles form. Skin sags.

Your need for rest or a
walk. You enjoy a friend's hug.

You make it through a pandemic.
You believe and hold the sacred—

Slavic ancestors from Poland
and Ukraine become guides.

Whale totem sings of the deep time.
Born from stardust, you grasp

new ideas in poems, performance,
and fiber art. I dress you in fun

textures and patterns. A pioneer,
you palm read the destiny of others.

SURRENDER

CEREMONY

SELF-DOUBT ERASED

Bear Goddess

My pilgrimage begins below the crescent moon.
I feel lost surrounded by the eyelids of dark trees.

Enter cave rooms. A bat darts. I scream.
Skulls and bones of bears neatly arranged.

Candlelight flickers. I place a bowl of peaches
and oranges. Then dip my hands in brackish

waters to sprinkle upon my offering.
Call upon Artio to banish my insecurities

and bring abundance. While my lips part,
I hear ancient Celtic songs. Self-doubt erased—

a ring of flames appears around my head
dancing ancestors joined by the goddess.

WISDOM

GENUINE

WATERS TO SPRINKLE
UPON MY OFFERING

Self-Forgiveness

I dance with Pele
through the fire door.
Burnt trees survive.
I wear their branches
as a crown of protection.
Tree of Life etches into my back.
A hollow place where leaves swirl.

I leave a community
for the pulse of the universe.
I don't have to apologize
or explain. The courage of my
ancestors when a meteor slices
mid-point through the Milky Way.
I am safe in constellation dark.

Linger. Breathe. Fall in love with myself.

OVERCOME

TRANSFORM

DANCING THROUGH THE FIRE DOOR

FALL IN LOVE WITH MYSELF

GENTLE

Nature's Alchemy

Sky meditates her gaze
to the heart of Earth.
Extracts and dispenses
her treasures. A conjuror?

Lovewater Earth struggles
while light is shaped
by imaginary gusts of wind—
recognizing Journey's voice
in each starling.

Sky thinks she's a jewel.
Observes birth and rebirth
of plants, rocks, and stones
all animated in their homage
as markers of time.

GUIDANCE

Belly Cry

The disgruntled went outside, cast a chain
around the sun and pulled it down. They lassoed

the pink moon and yanked it out of the sky.
Stars fell like tears. Earth Mother gasped

at the bombardment. The skin surrounding
the planet collapsed. Color faded on Tree of Life

as creation reversed. Confused animals and birds
clashed in the chaos. A cry rose from the belly

of every person as the world began to disappear.
The deafening sound wakened the roots of plants

which intertwined to hold the earth together.
Trees raised their branches to enfold the sky.

Green Tara and Lilith broke the chain and
unraveled the rope. Threw the sun and moon

back into orbit. Captured those who dared
to rip the cosmos.

*People, never forget the day your world
almost extinguished.*

DARING

CHAPTER TWO

AURA

GUIDED JOURNEYS

GUIDES: PASSION, SPEAK OUT 42 | ENERGY, OMENS 49 | PERSPECTIVE 55

COURAGE: STRENGTH 41 | CHALLENGE 43 | ROOTED, REACH 56

TREASURE: SEASON 38 | RESILIENCE 39 | COCOON 54 | SACRED 61 | TIMING 60

RITUAL: RECONNECT 40 | ROUGH, REBIRTH 50 | SLOWING 65

HORIZONS: KINDNESS 47 | PORTAL 51 | GO FORWARD 52

Water Goes Where it Wishes II

A slight breeze. Sunken treasure.
The Water Goddess
reflects on the still lake. Rainbows
receive their power from this magical mirror.

Volcanic fire sparks
up her spine
igniting all chakras. A protective

AURA

SEASON

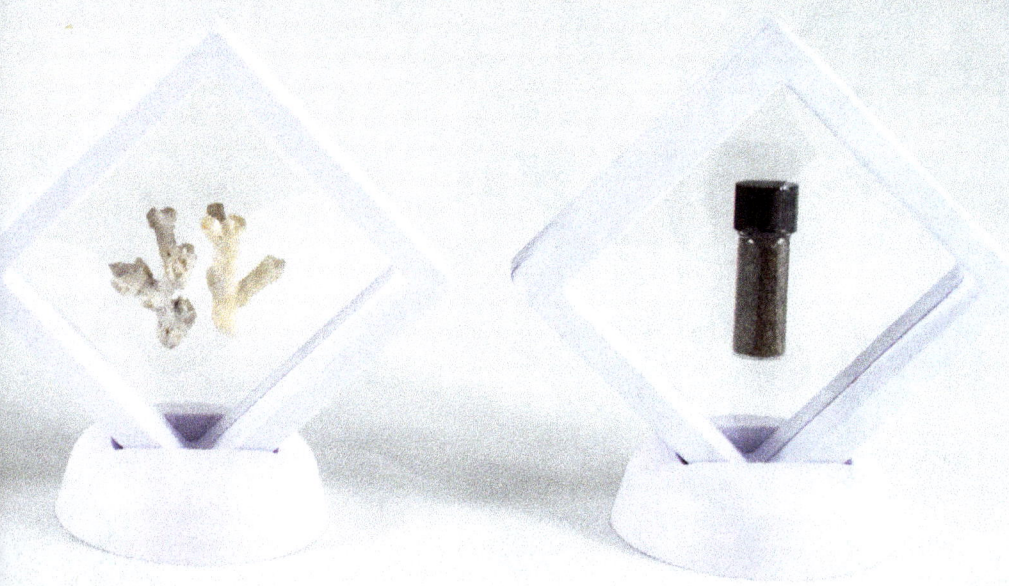

SPARKS UP HER SPINE

RESILIENCE

FIRE IN HER BELLY

STRENGTH

PASSION

TRANSITIONS

SPEAK OUT

DISCORD WITH PLANTS AND ANIMALS

of bedrock and bone

recordkeeper stoops over
her inner realm of
bedrock and organic matter

there's fire in her belly
She transitions from life to death

what is already dead inside?

Her bones contain
DNA sequences
of her ancestors

She listens to
each part of her body—

holy in community?
through the temple door—
path to the sacred grove

Devotion lost

many in discord with
plants and animals

is tenderness wrong?

CHALLENGE

of bedrock and bone II

She points to Demeter's Tree
Hangs mementos

of answered prayers
Fog dissipates

what is left?

MIST

DESTINY

GROWTH OF TALENTS

Connected

Witches dance under my aged, oak tree
branches for balance and strength.
Bronze leaves turn brittle and fall
from a great height. This morning
near my rough bark a child stumbles.
She holds a large and heavy rake.
Attempts to gather parts of me in crisp
air swirls. She sings of birds in a pie.
Black, long hair and wears a thick
orange coat with navy velvet trim.
She runs and jumps high into the
mountain of my leaves.
Crunch. Thud.

A landslide shifts amidst her screams
of delight. She hides from her grandfather.
He pretends to be angry. *You are making
more of a mess than helping*, he says.
She giggles. She's overseas
when he dies. Shedding tears
on a crowded bus leaning on the window.
I watch the growth and talents
of this woman. My leaves crisp over
and over above his rose garden.
Destiny recorded in my rings.
Autumn ritual.

KINDNESS

FLAME

FLOWS IN HER VEINS

CHANGE

ASTRAL BODY

Feldspar

Deep underground Basalt Goddess
wears seed pearls and licks honey from her fingers.
She's part volcanic glass. Feldspar
flows in her veins. Her astral body of light,
like vapor in the cliffs. Travels to the moon,
Mars, and Venus. Time means nothing.
Magma questions the shadows.

ENERGY

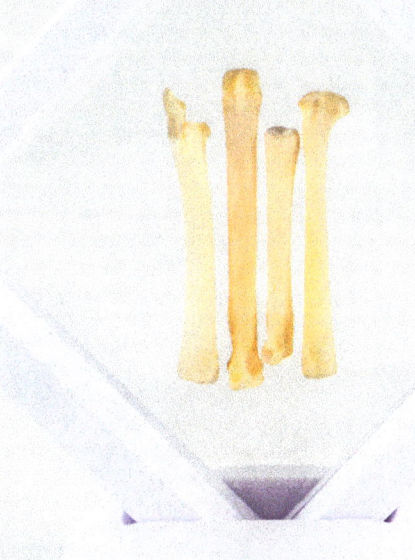

TIME MEANS NOTHING

OMENS

ROUGH

I MUST RETURN

REBIRTH

REMEMBER

Aquamarine

Basalt Goddess wonders if her organs
became fluid as a glacial river
beside craggy basalt columns—
hexagons formed
from melting snow. She explains,
I must return to the red planet.
Treks beneath the regolith surface
in ancient waters.
She births a mermaid with aquamarine hair—
vitreous luster, universal harmony symbol.
Glows in passageways. She tattoos a whale
on her child's arm to
remember earth's history.

PORTAL

Amethyst

Olympus Mons gently slopes. Basalt Goddess
digs for amethyst formed in hydrothermal veins.
Some radium required to grow in a place
of cloud-dust and ruins. Selkie creatures with
wrinkled skin summon her daughter.
They check her teeth with concern for cranial
damage. The young one stays
in their home of sea and smoke.
Mermaid as map connects worlds.

GO FORWARD

MERMAID AS MAP

REGENERATE

Warming

I'm sorry to keep you waiting.
From January my area steeps in snow.
For days it falls up to four feet. I walk
everywhere. Go inside an oak. I look up
to view veins, blood vessels, and a pulsing heart.
We vibrate as one.

Journey appears

Her home this constellation of tree.
She rotates upside down. Her long hair
merges as roots. My family ancestors' souls
reside next to each other. I catch
a bad case of influenza. I lack physical strength.
My lower back spirals in pain.
She asks what this ache needs.
I constrict in a fetal position.

Breathe

Deep

Goddess dazzles. Awakens warmer days.
April comes. Spring winks.
I chant for seeds to grow. Feel better. She calls her hawk

of beginnings and fire

He suspends in front of her face.
Then swoops. She senses slow
movements of my body.

PERSPECTIVE

ROOTED

STABILITY

REACH

CHANT FOR SEEDS TO GROW

SLOW MOVEMENTS

ALCHEMY

PUT INTO PLACE

NEW PATH

UNIQUE

SNOW-CHILLED BONES

SOLACE

NEW LIFE

SCAN THE HORIZON

SERENE

Dear Snowy Owl,

Your yellow eyes same size as mine
scanning the horizon. A thick coat of

feathers, regal as ancient cave paintings.
Windswept fields snow-chilled the bones of me.

You spot a small fire near the sea.
Turn toward the waves. I join you.

We sit with a woman Elder.

WIND

Dear Snowy Owl, II

Four Shells on the Ground Represent:

EARTH	FIRE	WATER	AIR
(ground)	(plants)	(sea)	(flight)

SACRED

GROUND

EARTH

GROW

FIRE

WATER

TIDES

FLY

AIR

Dear Snowy Owl, III

She cast herbs into the flame—
a ring of women dance above our heads.

Pulsations of shallow caribou skin
stretched one-side drum

What is your name?
She takes a long time to answer.

Eons, like the wisdom of Sedna.
Your dark beak opens. Shouts

a rough cry. Back home, I place secrets
of what matters in a cedar bark bowl.

      Yours always, Journey

SLOWING

CHAPTER THREE

TOME

GUIDED JOURNEYS

- **GRIEF:** COMFORT 68 | SPIRAL 71 | COURAGE 79 | MOVEMENT 93
- **MEMORY:** REFLECT, GAZE 72 | SUBTLE, VULNERABLE 75 | DESIRE 91
- **WISDOM:** SPEAK, FRIEND 73 | LISTEN 74 | DIVINE, PEACE 83
- **SILENCE:** WAIT, SONG 76 | HEAL 77 | SIGNS 84 | PRESENT 89
- **WILDERNESS:** LEARN 81 | THIRST, FOCUS 82 | CREATIVITY 86 | RISKS 90

Water Goes Where it Wishes III

Echolocation by whale—
An ice song opens a codex.
Letters of prayers
for the Water Goddess.
Sound waves wash her
Carry their guilt and shame.
She bears heaviness of the

TOME

COMFORT

SOUND WAVES WASH

HIDDEN

spiral open

sound of gongs and breath
as vibrations remind you
      her last sigh
when flowers bow and dance
the song of her laughter
      sound of gongs   sweet scent

now you see her face
      in magnolia flower—
sweet scent   laughter's song
her favorite perfume
      amber and nectarine
black and white photographs
depict wavy bob   wide skirt
      her future-self unknown
partial sight in one eye
      she watches the world askew
see her smile   this garden of grief
solitary tears curve   your face
her last sigh   the memory

TENDERNESS

garnet moon

reflects garden of grief
      partial sight   future-self
flowers bow and dance
she told you about ancestors
      immigrating from Ukraine
to New York   their belief
in a god whose name can't be spoken
      breath as vibration   solitary
the last gong struck with a felt beater
      spirals from the center
in a hollow pitch   the world askew

SPIRAL

REFLECT

BREATH AS VIBRATION

GAZE

FUTURE SELF

SECRETS OF THE DARK

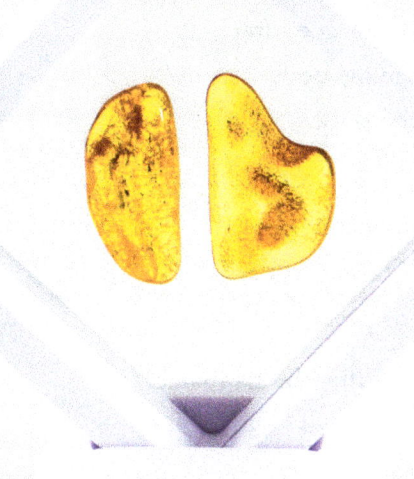

SPEAK

HERBS TO HEAL

FRIEND

Soundscapes

Apollo's snakes hiss in Casandra's ears
      with prophecies no one later
will believe   Chaos in my body
listens for secrets of the dark

I cup my ears
      Echoes map the landscape
red rock pinnacles   temple pillars
Goose honks wisdom at sunset

Witches chant   gather herbs to heal
ginger   calendula   fennel
      Plants grow from my legs
I paint their presence with my song

Vocal memories   of my lineage
whisper what was and returning
I massage my earlobes
      Wellness   calls   me

LISTEN

SUBTLE

THE WORLD BREATHES ME

WHISPER WHAT WAS

VULNERABLE

WAIT

BODY NEEDS REPAIR

SONG

VOCAL MEMORIES

I am more than my body

The netherworld holds
confusion   fear   loss
    my body needs   repair
I retreat inside my womb

Lanterns light the way
    I bathe   in calming waters
incense   prayer   not knowing
close my eyes and enter the silence

As the world breathes me
a bloodline   of the unseen
    underwater ancestors
intone   healing sounds   in unison

Aura shifts beyond my pain
    my soul conducts cosmic currents
I gather clothes   adorned   with stars
    Polaris glows   within

HEAL

SAFE

AURA SHIFTS

VISIBLE

ADORNED WITH STARS

Garden of Calm

Seek Deer Goddess crowned with a rack made of petrified wood for protection with calming calcite spots. She wanders. Never takes the same path. Be like a deer stalker in desperation, cunning—but not to kill her.

ACTION

Garden of Calm II

Return to the wilderness inside you. Use intuition to discern which river to follow. Select a stone who calls. Offer it to the water. Toss the rock into the eddies. Call the river's name out loud. Give thanks to Journey.

At dusk between the waking and the sleeping, discover the four-legged sage near the bank. A forest mother born of water and wind. Her fur of crimson columbines, bronze bells, and pinesap flowers like a garden of calm.

LEARN

THIRST

BORN OF WATER AND WIND

FOCUS

SHE DIRECTS ME

CRYSTALS NO FACETS

DIVINE

Garden of Calm III

Listen to her gentle voice. The goddess enlightens
to see obstacles as pebbles, not boulders. She directs me
to leave an old friend for the new. Ask one question.
I crochet the inquiry. Her kind eyes peer deep into mine.

Deer Goddess says, *What if flowers have no seeds or crystals no facets?*
Do not seek answers. Be the answer from within.

She disappears into the western yew leaving a balm
for wounds.

PEACE

SIGNS

REVEAL TIGER, PEACOCK, OR LOTUS

NATURE AND SIMPLICITY

HARMONY

Dear Fleeting Life,

In the beginning— ink strokes, the poetry of lines,
and the gaze of Kuan Yin in a reconstructed temple. A goddess
for my child-self. Scary guardians to keep away demons.
Lacquer and jade bowls. On a scroll, a sage sits near a hut, small
against vast mountains and waterfalls. Other paintings reveal
tiger, peacock, or lotus. Purple iris on golden screen
waver through me.

As a youth, I teach myself watercolor painting.
I copy Asian paintings on rice paper. A geisha looks at me
in her flowing robes. I envision being a princess
in a Chinese court. An ancestor shows me how to understand a
scroll as a story from bottom to top. Nature and simplicity my
anchors. The goddess of compassion assures me I am still.

As an adult, I write a story. An unborn child visits
her grandmother in a past life. They celebrate a traditional
tea ceremony in winter. Then discuss life to come
and an unmarked grave. One stroke in black ink, an enso scroll
hangs over hot steam. I wear a red kimono with a white butterfly.
Pretend I am under cherry tree blossoms. The first messengers
of spring.

CREATIVITY

LOYALTY

HOW TO UNDERSTAND

WRITE A STORY

PLAY

DUALITY

LIGHT AND SHADOW SIDES

FLOW

SHE OVERSEES

rose, goddess, bee, moon

moon knows about the bees
even if they sleep under her watch
roses share secrets with Journey
she oversees a fertile ground
light and shadow sides of her
protect against depression as honey melts

PRESENT

RISKS

WOVE MEDICINE

Ix Chel

Jaguar crone chases the sun
Her lover disappears beneath
Tides she controls

Long ago, Ix Chel and Itzamna
Wove medicine—
All bodies of water into existence and
Scorpion, Turtle, Snake constellations

Cenote their favorite place to rest
Above gateway to underworld

>Alux lured this lizard
>Into thunder spirit portal

>Afraid constant rays
>Brittled jungle leaves

>Illusion of winds
>Rumbled wisdom
>Electrifying shifts

Creatrix now separated
Light and dark cycles
First Mother remembers
His fiery touch

DESIRE

EXPECTATION

THUNDER SPIRIT PORTAL

INSPIRE

RUMBLED WISDOM

CHAPTER FOUR
EVOLVE

GUIDED JOURNEYS

- **IDENTITY:** PERMISSION 96 | SUBCONSCIOUS 97 | HOPE, RECHARGE 119 | AFFINITY 122

- **STRUGGLE:** PILGRIMAGE 98 | UNCLUTTER, UNDERTOW 99 | RITUAL 116 | CONJURE, ALIGN 118

- **HEALING:** GIFTS 101 | RECOVERY 103 | UNCONDITIONAL 110 | QUIET, CONNECT 112 | RELAX 123

- **WITNESS:** NOURISH 102 | CONVERSATION 113 | CENTER, NATURE 121

- **RELEASE:** FIERY ENERGY 104 | ADJUST, PROTECT 108 | INTENTION 109 | LOST 120

PERMISSION

FLUID VOICE

Water Goes Where it Wishes IV

Under crescent moon
Water Goddess converses
in a fluid voice with sea urchin
who walks slowly using tube feet
avoiding starfish and wolf eel.
The goddess wonders how she will

EVOLVE

SUBCONSCIOUS

In the Belly of a Canoe

I traverse the lower world
      cocooned in a canoe
Shamanic drumbeats in snake rhythm
take me far back to look forward
Map unfolds in a parallel universe

      In a trance
turquoise waters surround
Sea turtle glides unseen among
wavering seaweed
Your presence vibrates my inner core
Mark-making humanity scribes your
shell like cracks in the mud

Inside my belly unbroken waves of water
and sand burn through ashen undertow
      Sucked under,
I am suddenly washed by
jealousy, helplessness, and shame
You say, *Don't struggle against the tide*

PILGRIMAGE

UNCLUTTER

MAP UNFOLDS

SUDDENLY WASHED

UNDERTOW

GIFTS

POINT THE PROW

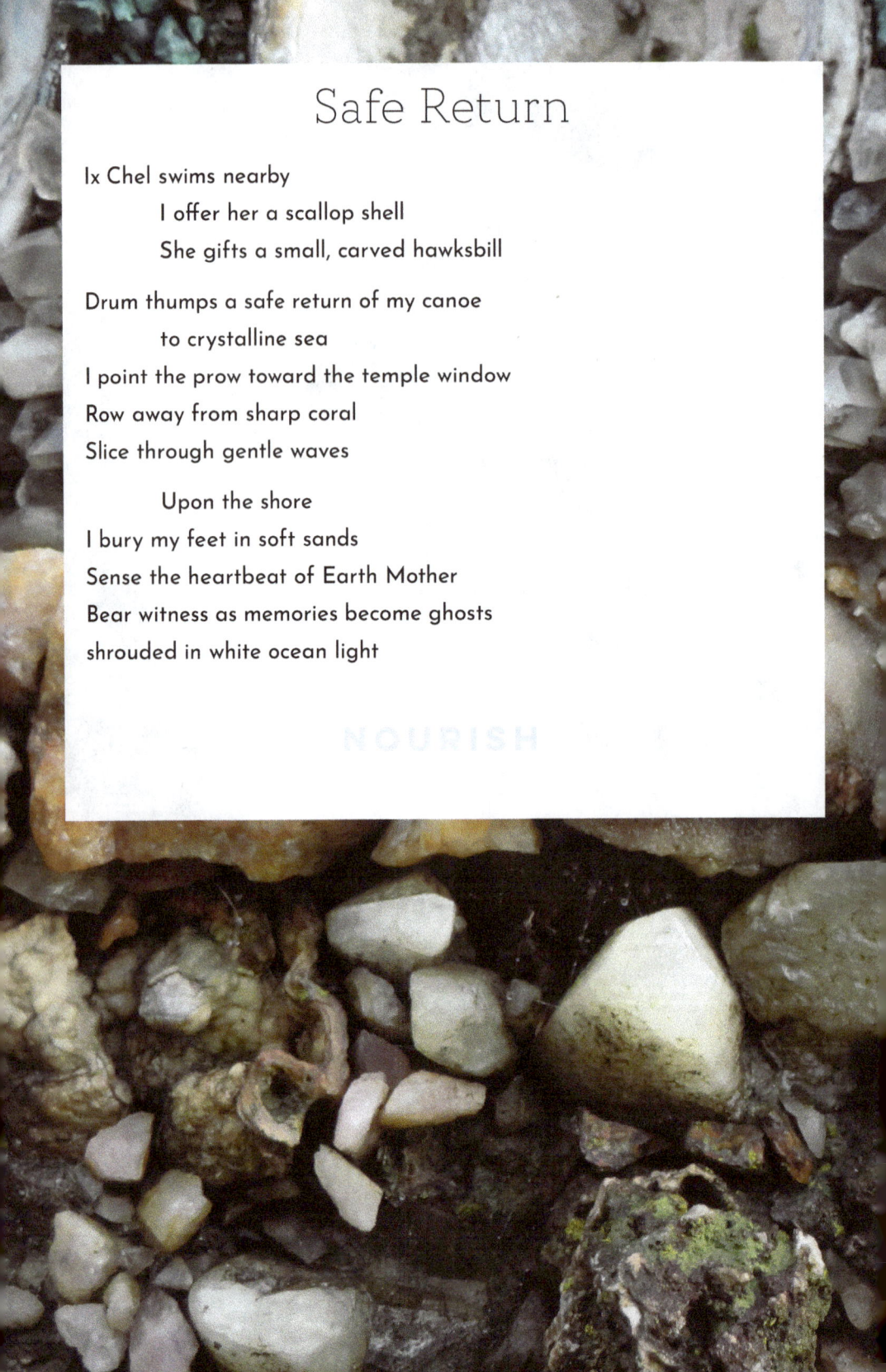

Safe Return

Ix Chel swims nearby
      I offer her a scallop shell
        She gifts a small, carved hawksbill

Drum thumps a safe return of my canoe
      to crystalline sea
I point the prow toward the temple window
Row away from sharp coral
Slice through gentle waves

      Upon the shore
I bury my feet in soft sands
Sense the heartbeat of Earth Mother
Bear witness as memories become ghosts
shrouded in white ocean light

NOURISH

HOME: Winter Crossroads

Firewood smoke snakes across the canyon.
Birds chatter. A golden weave of leaves
vibrate in twilight's shiver. Snowmelt gushes.
A gurgling stream like waters in my belly.

> The torn edges of fear, loss, despair
> devour the broken bowl of my body.

Dhumavati, crone of letting go, instructs:
Get rid of 27 objects for each of nine days.
I sort through jewelry, books, and clothes.
Say, *thank you.* Liberate the memories.

> Release who I was
> to become who I am.

Hecate encourages be a silent witness.
Strong shelter for my words. A home aglow.
In my room, I sweep a path under a bridge
for glass fish in a miniature Japanese sand garden.

> Add stone, shell, and coral.
> A map of a sacred solstice site.

FIERY ENERGY

ADJUST

RELEASE

PROTECT

SUN IN MY HORNS

THIS THRESHOLD

INTENTION

Gift Giver

I am the gift giver
with the sun in my horns

A female shaman
of Mongol blood

I wear antlers
tree of life symbol

On the night of the Mothers
stars cover my body

Healings in flight
for my tribe

This threshold—
solstice dark

shifts solar rebirth
deep time stories

UNCONDITIONAL

HONEST

SOLSTICE DARK

DEEP TIME

LINEAGE

QUIET

COLLECTIVE MEMORY

CONNECT

PLACE MY PALMS

Select Another Possibility

When I come upon the large rock bowl
    smoothly carved atop a granite boulder,

When I sense the collective memory of a wise woman
    where rock shadow is her silhouette,

When I place my palms in the center depression,
    my mind hears clearing,

When I picture a quartz crystal
    I also sense release, shed, start over,

How loud rock-climbing voices
    hover over me,

Wait until you get to the other side, he shouts,
    disturbing desert silence,

Sublime messages from everywhere.

CONVERSATION

RESPECT

SUBLIME MESSAGES

Landscape Inside Mother Earth

Pele shakes the turtle rattle. Sharp jolts.
She dances within the landscape of my chest.

My ribs open to access my heart.
But gopher digs nearby
and duck sleeps on a log oblivious.

Blue heron squawks. Disappears.
Oak tree hugs boulders
in a sturdy niche. Stones erode.

Pele embraces me. Cottonwood fluff
calm in still air. Lower pine spine burnt.
Needled branches spindle to

protect young maple. Her face hidden.
She conjures wisdom stories.
They appear as forest flames
on my lungs of silent waters.

RITUAL

Chaparral Resurgence

    after heat shock
I chew Mormon tea stalk   freshness explodes
      helps me breathe
I stand in a circle of entwined trees
burnt manzanita branches   spiral
sun fires through peeled bark
holds past life   of somatic winds

whispering bells shake their heads
aromatic yerba santa   dots the hillside
    oak bushes cluster under barren trunks
      buckwheat disappears
tips of yucca bloom

BREATHE

CONJURE

MY RIBS OPEN

ALIGN

LUNGS OF SILENT WATERS

FRESHNESS EXPLODES

HOPE

HOLDS A PAST LIFE

RECHARGE

Under Blood Moon

Nature goes fallow
      raven Morrigan flies by during
morning prayers   requires boldness
I let go   nourish   the dark

Black sand leeches from inside me
settles in   sea depths
     Bioluminescent anglerfish
jagged teeth   devours   my anxious

thoughts   I am weak and depleted
     embrace the angry monster
Sparks   sear down my spine
accept   day and night   of self

Frankincense and myrrh needle
my skin   body   first home
    lunar wisdom remembers
how to heal   deep breath   gravity

LOST

CENTER

ACCEPT DAY AND NIGHT

LUNAR WISDOM

NATURE

View Down the Path

Walk with my friend next to yucca
as early morning heat presses.
Ahead, on the dusty road
smooth stone rests in the center.
She says, Take it, it's for you.
The dark rock fits in my palm,
holds weight.

Perhaps a Power Stone?

Mother Earth has offered a gift.
Introduce myself, bless, and ask
if the stone wants to work
with me? Returning home,
I place it by my bed.

Wind walker

brings comfort when I don't
feel well. In candlelight,
my red bones unshackled
made sacred closing the gap
between me and myself.

AFFINITY

View Down the Path II

Consider: roots of old trees
on a lakeshore keep the soil
from tumbling and sinking
to the bottom or
blowing across water
like skipping stones.
Journey rubs the Power Stone
across my shoulders and
spine before going to sleep.

RELAX

EPILOGUE

GUIDED JOURNEYS

REST: SHRINE 126 | SYMPATHY 127 | GLOW 128 | BLOOM 129

DIARY: RUMINATE 130 | MEMORIES, ACCUMULATION 131 | DISCERN 133

Pause

Journey enters the temple grounds where Kuan Yin resides
next to the large lotus fountain. Branches and leaves
of an aged bodhi tree reflect in the pool.
Steps like an altar begin with a dragon sculpture,
then a row of stones, three buddhas next,
and two mourning doves crown the scene. Going indoors,
a community fills the room of lace blouses, wrapped skirts,
and woven shirts. Journey sits cross-legged on a patterned rug
in fossilized weariness. Monks chant in a canyon of language.
Voices in her head try to drown their song. She struggles
to focus on their resonant sound. Then energy buzzes
throughout her body. Her heart stops believing lies.
Outside, hands mold a small mountain of dirt
blanketed with yellow, pink, and orange flowers,
She plants incense into the fertile soil. A smoky prayer
to remember her ancestors as a new tiger year blooms.
Dividing rice into six portions, Journey carefully places
the grains in each monk's silver vessel. Donates alms
into saffron bags. They sit in a row. She dips her carnation
white with red tips into a cup of water, rubs the flower
along the lifelines of their cupped hands. Water soaks their robes.
Closed eyes, but one looks at her for a moment. Last monk
in line traveled all the way from Cambodia. Wears a darker robe
of fine, woven burgundy threads like brown jasper.

Near her
Turtle reminds
pause in bodhi shadows

GLOW

SMOKY PRAYER

Mark Time

Ursa Major in northern sky
Greater she-bear once a nymph
      home in healing springs
tangle of wilderness   stirs

      Bear asks her to digest doubts
Journey sits   straight spine
waning crescent of unknowing
      listens waits imagines

She prays many names
         of sacred mother
      faces her mortality
black willow   frog totem   speak

Waterfall douses fire stones   of fears
        connects   floats   rests
She keeps   cryptic diary
      from water's point of view

RUMINATE

MEMORIES

DIGEST DOUBTS

ACCUMULATION

FIRESTONES OF FEAR

OBJECTS

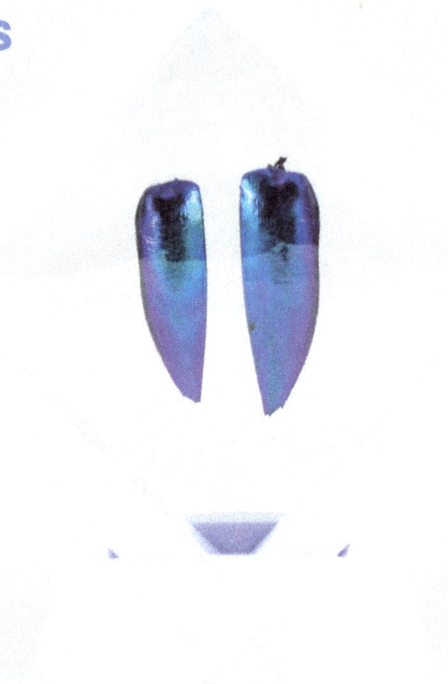

CHARMS THE WIND

IDENTITY

DECIDES TO FORGET

Beginning Again

Feathers and bones in her hands—
decaying antlers enrich the earth
primal temptress charms the winds
a sparrow deprived of the oxygen of myth.

Journey journals during the art
poetry meditation. Each breath
marks a page. She says goodbye
to her stream. Creates traction
written from the womb.

Fire in the third chakra,
a mandala of trees and the sun's aura,
burns what she decides to forget.

Beginning again, across her
shoulders, seeds fan
into passion flowers.
She outlines with gutta
flames of rebirth.

Before rains fall and grasses reach,
she is formless.

DISCERN

Notes

- *Soundscapes*: Inspired by *Wild Geese* Foresta Collective Dojo
- *Mark Time*: Story of Callisto, Greek nymph
- *In the Belly of a Canoe* and *Ix Chel*: inspired by my trip to the Yucatán, Mexico
- *Beginning Again*: the line, "deprived of the oxygen of myth" by Caryn Davidson, used with permission

Acknowledgments

- *A Moon of One's Own*: Soundscapes
- *California Quarterly*: View Down the Path, In the Belly of a Canoe
- *Cholla Needles Press*: rose, antlers, goddess, bee, moon
- *Crone Lit: A Collection of Crone Literature*: HOME: Winter Crossroads Ethel Zine: Bear Goddess
- *Innate DIVINITY books Anthology*: "A Case for the Personhood of Trees;" of bedrock and bone, Self-Forgiveness, Chapparal Resurgence, Landscape inside Mother Earth
- *Lothlorien Poetry Journal*: Mark Time, Dear Snowy Owl
- *Mythos Magazine*: Ix Chel, Under Blood Moon
- *OyeDrum*: Gift Giver
- *SeedBroadcast*: Garden of Calm, Warming
- *Shoebox PR•Art and Cake* - "Call & Response Round I:" Belly Cry
- *Spectrum 25 - Fall Issue*: Connected
- *The Journal of Radical Wonder*: Select Another Possibility, I am more than my body, Pause, Dear Rough Emerald
- *The World of Myth Magazine*: Water Goes Where It Wishes
- *Verse-Virtual*: Beginning Again
- *Wild Roof Journal*: Glowing Stones

Many thanks to Heather Rinne whose photographs from The Shrine of the Grotto of the Redemption, West Bend, IA started the idea for this book, and her input on the images. I am grateful for A.E. Van Fleet who spent countless hours discussing the meaning of his sculpture symbols to pair them with my poems. Thank you to my desert critique group for editing the poems. Gratitude to Jenny Drai for looking at the first chapter for concept and editing through Black Lawrence Press. Thanks to Nauset Press and Karyn Kloumann, publisher, for bringing this book of journeys to life and for believing in me.

Artist Biographies

As part of her BFA from Cal Poly Pomona, **Heather Rinne** studied film and digital photography. Her passion is black and white film. She has a collection of 11 (and counting!) vintage cameras, most in working order. Heather has shown her work at the Brand Library & Art Center (Glendale, CA), Cal Poly Pomona, SCA Project Gallery (Pomona, CA), the National Orange Show Art Gallery (San Bernardino, CA) and the Long Beach Public Library. Her photos have been published in *Inlandia: A Literary Journal* and *The Chaffey Review*. She was a finalist for the 24/1 photo essay contest hosted by The Music Center in Los Angeles and was awarded 2nd place in the Spencer Chamber of Commerce Spring Photo Contest. Heather uses photography to document her travels. www.heatherfeatherdesign.com

A.E. Van Fleet is an interdisciplinary artist and graphic designer living in Fullerton, Calif. He received both his BA in Graphic Design and his MFA in Studio Art and Design from California State University, San Bernardino. Van Fleet unites his influences from pop culture and esotericism to works that challenge traditional binary categorizations in western art and culture, using unusual mediums while attempting to demystify the veil that separates the experiential from the transcendent. He has participated in several group exhibitions at venues like the Little Gallery of San Bernardino, Robert and Frances Museum of Art, dA Center for the Arts, National Orange Show Art Gallery, and the Aquarium of the Pacific, Long Beach. He is the owner of Fine Nerdistry Prints, an Etsy shop specializing in archival pigment prints featuring handmade textures made from masking tape and shoe polish. www.aevanfleet.com

www.ingramcontent.com/pod-product-compliance
Lightning Source LLC
Chambersburg PA
CBHW070547090426
42735CB00013B/3091